*The Story of the*
STAR-SPANGLED BANNER

The Widow Pickersgill made it. Her daughter Caroline helped her, because the flag with its fifteen stars must be flying over Fort McHenry before the British fleet attacked it. It was August 24, 1814, in Baltimore.

So begins the story in which Francis Scott Key and his friend, John Skinner, slip out of the harbor in a small boat flying a white flag. Their mission is to intercept the British flagship and beg for the release of Dr. William Beanes, who is a prisoner of war.

Their errand is successful, but only after they spend a wild night as prisoners themselves while the British bombard the fort and threaten to burn the city.

The welcome sight of the flag at dawn inspires Mr. Key to jot down the lines of a poem on an old envelope. He called it *The Defense of Fort McHenry*. We call it *The Star-Spangled Banner*.

This is the story of the dramatic events that led a man to write a poem and of what has happened to it.

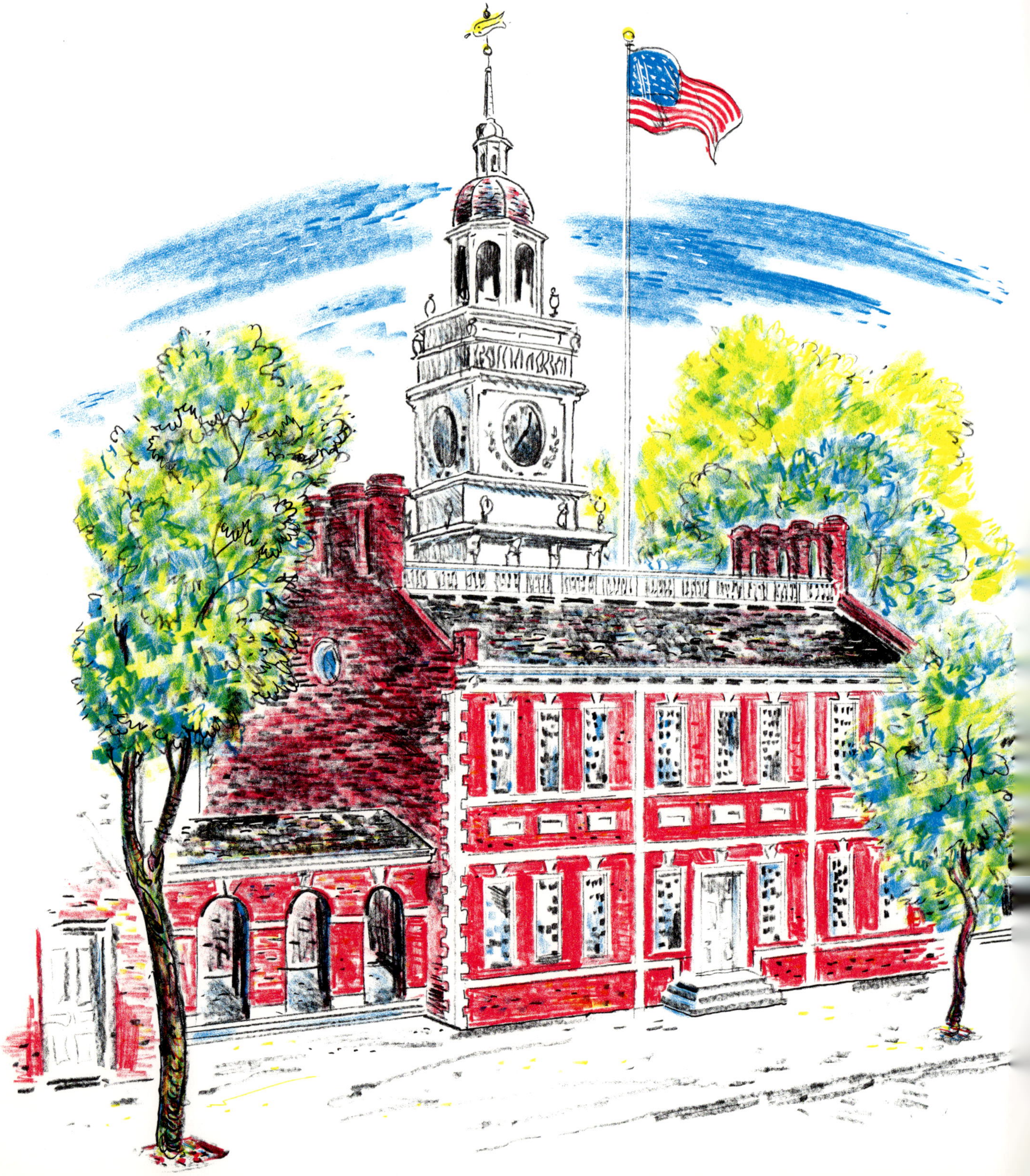

The story of the
# STAR-SPANGLED BANNER

By Natalie Miller

Illustrations by George Wilde

CHILDRENS PRESS, Chicago

Library of Congress Catalog Card Number: 65-1221

Copyright © 1965, Childrens Press

All rights reserved. Printed in the U.S.A.

Published simultaneously in Canada

29 R 93 92 91

LIBRARY
HOLBEIN SCH.
MT. HOLLY, NJ.

Caroline Pickersgill was tired. It was way past her bedtime. All day long she had been helping her mother sew together a huge American flag. It was so large that the only place in Baltimore to spread it out was on the floor of the local brewery. There was still much to be done before the candles sputtered out and they could go home.

The Widow Pickersgill made flags to support herself and her twelve-year-old daughter. In ordinary times she would have done all the work alone. But the summer of 1814 was no ordinary time. America was at war with Great Britain.

Terrible rumors had reached Baltimore that a few nights before, on August 24, the enemy had marched into Washington and burned all the important government buildings. They had even burned the President's house.

The British admiral who carried the soldiers from place to place on his ships, boasted he would do the same to Baltimore.

No one in Baltimore knew when the enemy would strike but they planned to be ready.

Caroline could hear wagons outside the window rumbling toward Fort McHenry with things for the soldiers who would guard the entrance to the harbor. She could hear the clang of shovels as sweating men dug trenches around the city.

The flag must be flying over Fort McHenry before the enemy fleet appeared in the bay. That might be tomorrow! Caroline rubbed her eyes and kept on sewing.

A few days later, on September 2, as the great new flag flapped gently in the breeze, a small gray boat slipped quietly out of Baltimore harbor and passed the Fort. It had no name or number and it flew a white flag.

The two Americans on board looked back at the fort with its new flag—fifteen stripes, and fifteen stars on a field of bright blue.

"I like the size of that flag," said the young lawyer, Francis Scott Key. "It will let the enemy know that Baltimore is proud of its country."

He had no idea of how important the size of that same flag would be to him a few days later.

Key watched the flag until it was out of sight but his companion, John Skinner, looked over the bay in search of the enemy fleet.

The two men had orders from President Madison to try to beg the freedom of Dr. William Beanes, a good friend of Mr. Key. He was a prisoner held aboard a British warship.

Two or three days later and many miles down Chesapeake Bay they saw the masts of the enemy fleet against the sky.

"There must be fifty ships," said Key.

"Nearer seventy," replied Skinner who knew more about ships.

"I hope we get back in time to warn Baltimore," said Key.

Their little boat bounced like a tiny gray chip among the giant vessels. It bobbed its way right to the admiral's flagship.

The British sailors lowered a rope ladder when they saw the white flag of truce, and the two men climbed aboard.

The admiral of the fleet and General Ross of the army were both there and greeted them politely. But when Key asked for his friend's freedom, they frowned coldly and refused.

Then Key gave them letters from wounded British officers telling how kindly Dr. Beanes had treated them. At last General Ross, whose soldiers had taken him prisoner, agreed to free the elderly gentleman.

"But not until after our attack on Baltimore," said Admiral Cochrane. "We cannot risk having you go back and give information about what you have seen here."

The admiral's own ship was crowded with British army officers, so the Americans were put aboard a smaller British ship, the *Surprise*.

They watched helplessly as sailors tied their little boat under the stern of the frigate and took away the sails. Now there was no way they could escape to warn Baltimore.

For six days the "guests" wandered about the deck of the *Surprise* as the fleet slowly made its way up Chesapeake Bay.

Key thought often about the big flag flying over Fort McHenry. To know that Baltimore was getting ready for a battle gave him comfort.

When the fleet reached North Point he could see the flag flying high over the low-lying fort. Its colors were strong and true.

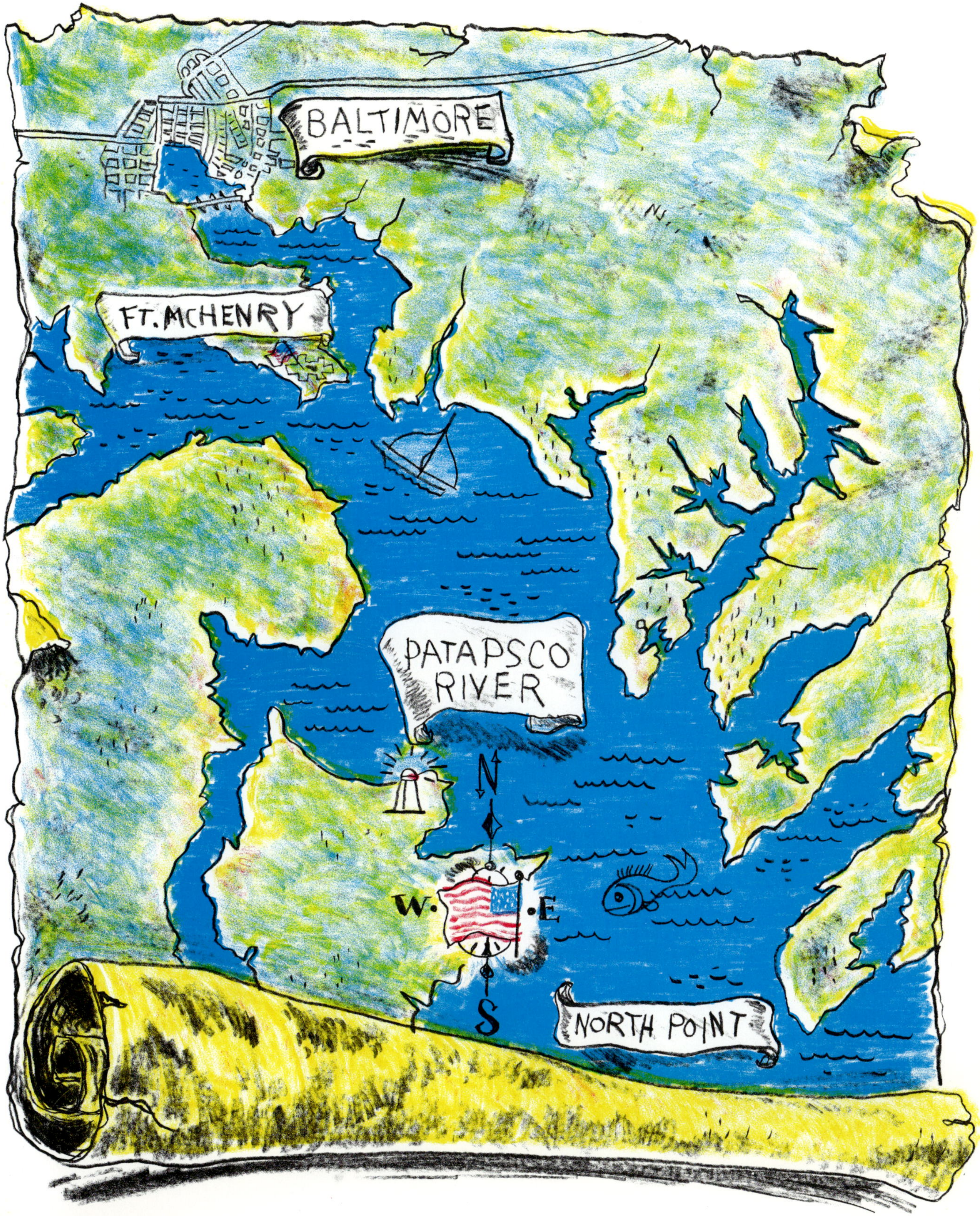
BALTIMORE
FT. MCHENRY
PATAPSCO RIVER
N
W
E
S
NORTH POINT

On Sunday morning, September 12, the Americans, including Dr. Beanes, watched hundreds of British soldiers being sent ashore.

Before dawn the next morning the ships opened fire on Fort McHenry. The broadsides from the *Surprise* churned the water angrily.

The battle lasted all day and far into the night. Thick smoke blotted the view. Their nostrils burned with the smell of gunpowder and their heads throbbed with the constant booming.

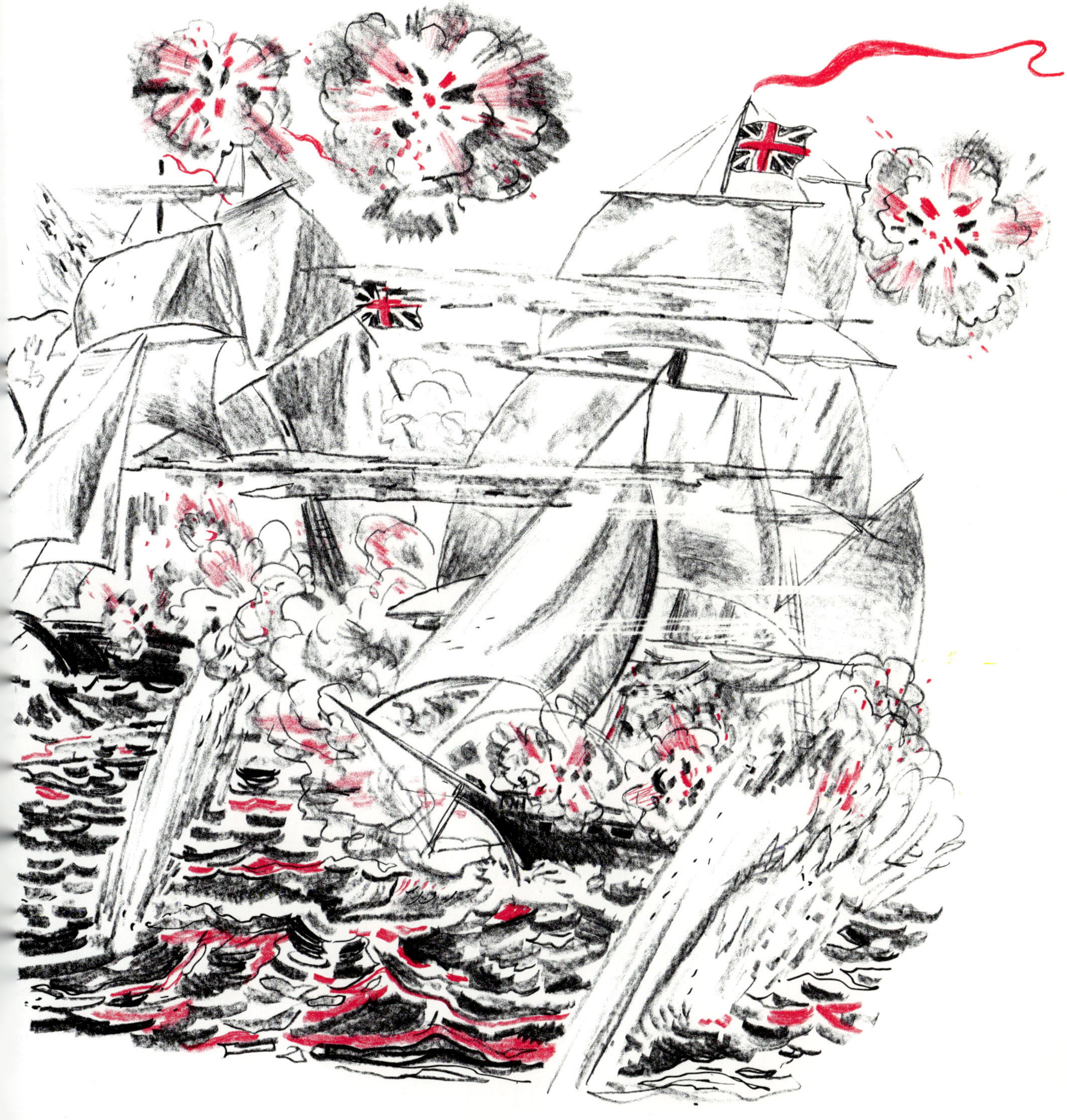

Suddenly all was quiet. It was midnight black. They could see nothing. Had the fort surrendered? They paced the deck—waiting, waiting.

Francis Scott Key had written many poems. During the dark hours of waiting, words and lines marched in his mind.

When dawn's early light colored the sky, the men could make out the flag, still waving proudly. Tears of relief filled their eyes.

Key pulled an old envelope from his pocket. He began writing all the things he had thought about during the night. There was not room on the paper to write everything he felt in his heart, but he jotted down his main ideas.

He was so busy he didn't notice that the British soldiers were being brought back to the ships.

When the last troops had returned, sailors handed down their sails and they were free to go. Without delay they set sail upstream for the five-mile trip to Baltimore.

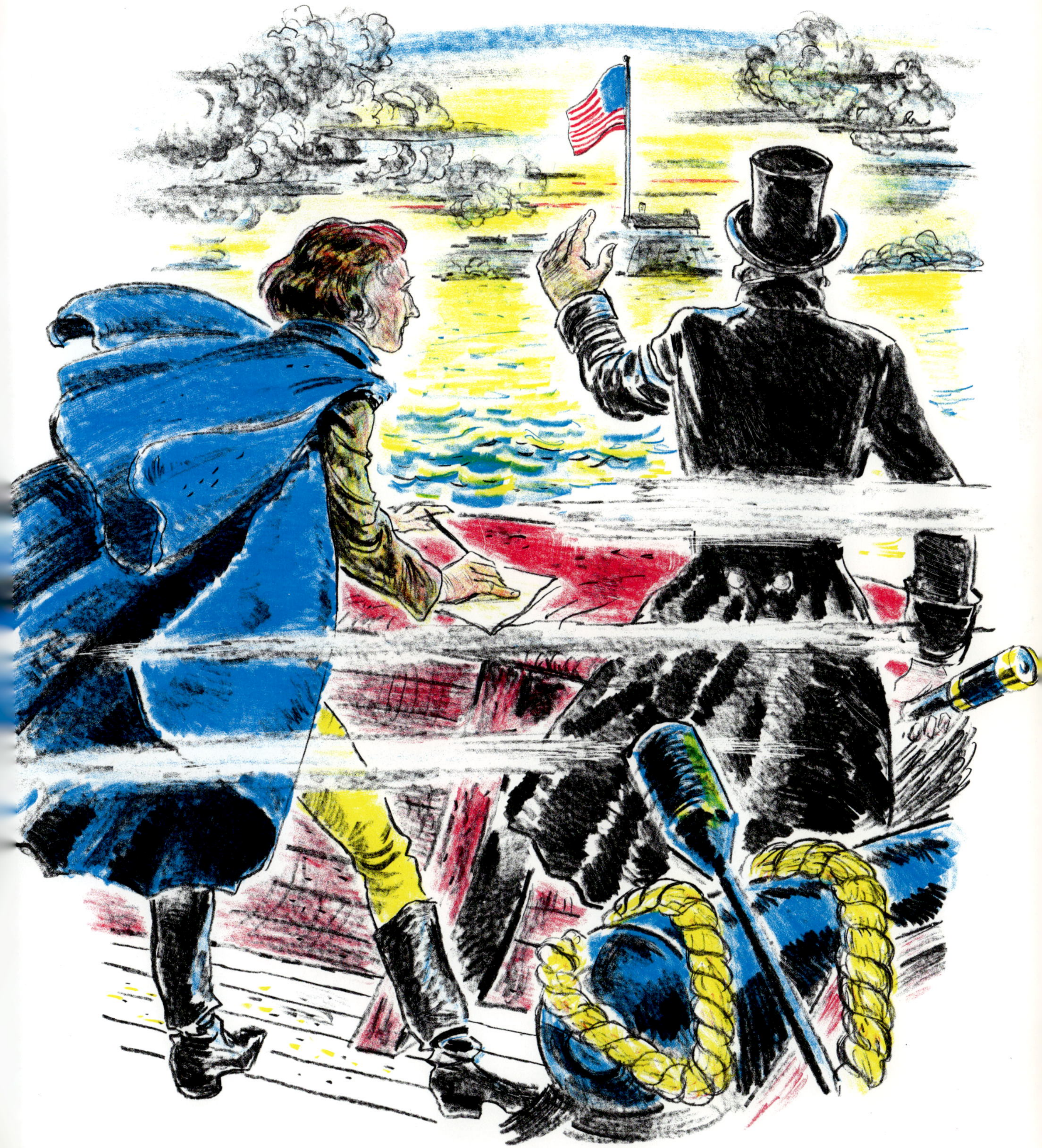

They went at once to the Old Fountain Inn, too tired to join the crowds of merrymakers in the streets.

Dr. Beanes and John Skinner went to sleep at once, but Francis Scott Key called for ink and paper.

He set to work copying in his neat handwriting the words he had written on the envelope. He changed some of the words and sentences until they sounded as he wanted them to.

As soon as he had finished he tossed down the pen. He fell on the bed and into a deep sleep as the others had done.

The paper he left carelessly lying on the desk would one day be sold for over $24,000.

The next morning he hunted up his brother-in-law, Judge J. H. Nicholson, and showed him the poem.

The Judge was so impressed with it he took it to the printing office of the *Baltimore American,* a newspaper.

The only one there was fourteen-year-old Samuel Sands who had been left to tend the office while the men were away fighting.

"I'll be glad to run it off in handbills for you," offered Sam reading it over. "Does it have a title?"

"Call it *The Defense of Fort M'Henry,*" said the Judge.

Sam was happy to have something to do.

A note on the poem said, "Tune: *To Anacreon in Heaven.*" Sam hummed it as he worked. It was a well-known tune.

He wondered who had written the poem for there was no name on the neat paper.

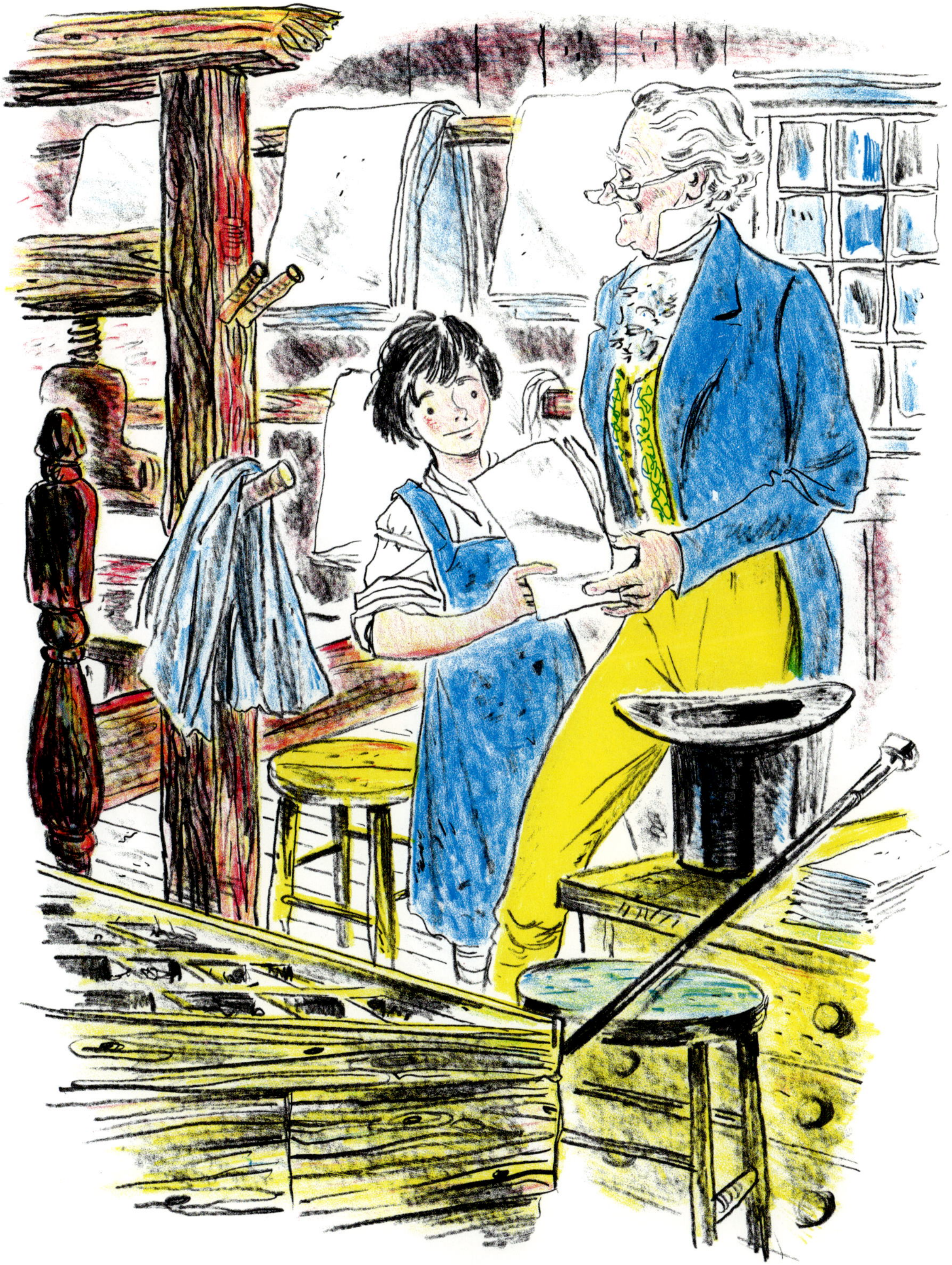

By the next morning copies of the song had been passed out all over town. Soldiers returning from the trenches read it. Housewives sang it softly as they went about their chores. Men in coffee houses and taverns sang it in harmony.

Key did not wait to see how people liked it. He put a few copies in his pocket for his family and took the earliest coach going toward home.

As soon as the Baltimore newspapers started printing again, they published *The Defense of Fort M'Henry.* Papers in other cities copied it. They changed the title to *The Star-Spangled Banner.*

Key was pleased to hear it sung so often and flattered when it was printed in song books. It did not bother him that his name seldom appeared as the author. He did not think its popularity would last.

He had written a song for that same tune ten years before, honoring the soldiers returning from Tripoli. It had quickly been forgotten.

When he died almost thirty years later he still believed his *Star-Spangled Banner* would not live.

It would have surprised him if he could have known that his song was sung as much as *Yankee Doodle* and *America* during the Civil War.

Some southern troops tried to rewrite the words making fun of the North, but Key's words and the tune were so much a part of each other they could not be separated. The song became more popular than ever.

During the Spanish-American War in 1898, Admiral Dewey asked that *The Star-Spangled Banner* be used for ceremonial occasions in the navy.

After he captured the Spanish fleet in Manila Bay on the other side of the world, his navy band played the song as his men stood at attention.

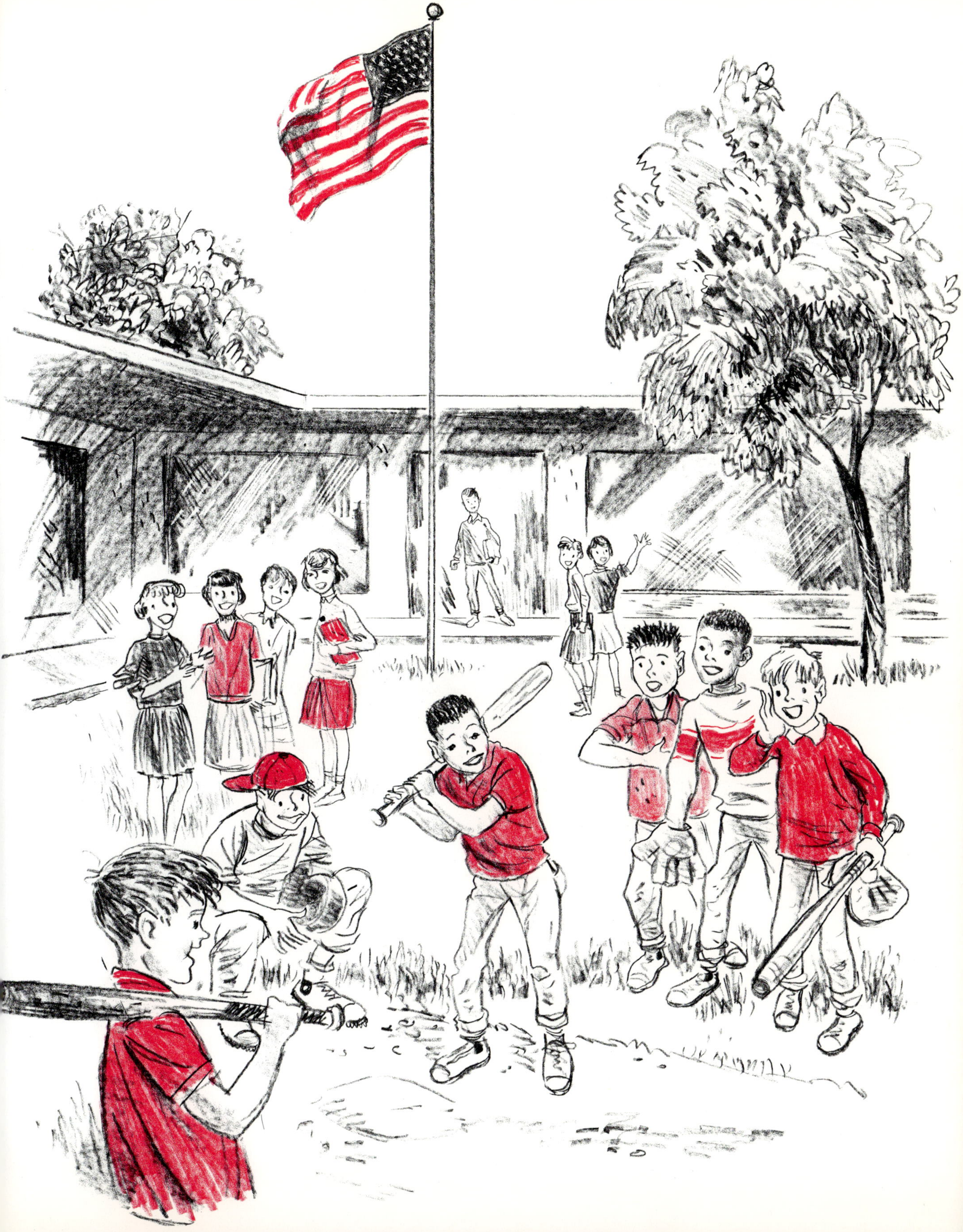

# The Star-Spangled Banner
*By Francis Scott Key*

O say, can you see, by the dawn's early
    light,
What so proudly we hailed at the twilight's
    last gleaming?
Whose broad stripes and bright stars, through
    the perilous fight,
O'er the ramparts we watched, were so
    gallantly streaming!
And the rockets' red glare, the bombs
    bursting in air,
Gave proof through the night that our flag
    was still there:
    O say, does that star-spangled banner yet
        wave
    O'er the land of the free and the home of
        the brave?

On the shore, dimly seen through the mists
    of the deep,
Where the foe's haughty host in dread silence
    reposes.
What is that which the breeze, o'er the
    towering steep,
As it fitfully blows, now conceals, now
    discloses?
Now it catches the gleam of the morning's
    first beam,
In full glory reflected now shines on the
    stream:
    'Tis the star-spangled banner! O long may
        it wave
    O'er the land of the free and the home of
        the brave!

THE BETSY ROSS FLAG
(1777)

AMERICAN FLAG IN THE TIME
OF THE WIDOW PICKERSGILL
(1794-1818)

And where is that band who so vauntingly
    swore
That the havoc of war and the battle's
    confusion
A home and a country should leave us no
    more?
Their blood has washed out their foul
    footsteps' pollution.
No refuge could save the hireling and slave
From the terror of flight, or the gloom of
    the grave:
    And the star-spangled banner in triumph
        doth wave
    O'er the land of the free and the home of
        the brave!

Oh! thus be it ever, when freemen shall
    stand
Between their loved homes and the war's
    desolation!
Blest with victory and peace, may the
    heaven-rescued land
Praise the Power that hath made and
    preserved us a nation.
Then conquer we must, for our cause it is
    just,
And this be our motto: "In God is our trust."
    And the star-spangled banner in triumph
        shall wave
    O'er the land of the free and the home of
        the brave!

AMERICAN FLAG
(1818)

AMERICAN FLAG
(1960)